SUPER

and the
NIGHTMARE
on
NEPTUNE

A SOLAR SYSTEM
ADVENTURE

by Steve Korté
illustrated by Dario Brizuela

Superman created by Jerry Siegel and Joe Shuster
by special arrangement with the Jerry Siegel family

Consultant:
Steve Kortenkamp, PhD
Associate Professor of Practice
Lunar and Planetary Lab
University of Arizona
Tucson, Arizona

CAPSTONE PRESS
a capstone imprint

At S.T.A.R. Labs, Professor Emil Hamilton uses his computer to monitor the air quality of Metropolis.

Suddenly, he sees an object streak across his screen. It's entering Earth's atmosphere, but it's not an asteroid or a comet.

"That looks like a spacecraft," says Hamilton with astonishment. "It's heading straight toward the Metropolis harbor!"

SPLASH!

The metal spacecraft sinks into the harbor.

"I'd better call Superman!" exclaims Hamilton.

Moments later, the mighty hero Superman arrives and dives into the harbor. Suddenly, the Man of Steel rises to the surface, trapped in Doomsday's massive arms.

Doomsday is one of the Man of Steel's deadliest enemies. The super-strong creature was created as the ultimate killing machine. His skin is tipped with razor-sharp bones that can injure even Superman.

Superman uses his super-strength to flip Doomsday through the air.

CRASH!

The creature lands in the middle of a highway at the edge of the harbor. Two cars screech to a stop next to the monster. The drivers of both vehicles jump out of the cars and run for safety.

Doomsday growls and quickly jumps to his feet. He grabs the two cars, lifts them above his head, and flings them at Superman.

ZAAAP!

Red-hot lasers shoot out of Superman's eyes. His heat-vision melts the cars in midair.

Superman flies straight toward Doomsday.

BLAM!

Superman's fists crash against Doomsday's head. The monster falls to the ground. Doomsday is unconscious, but Superman knows he won't be out for long.

Superman uses a small radio device in his cape to speak with Hamilton.

"Professor, I need to get Doomsday far from Earth," he says. "I'm going to take him to the farthest planet in our solar system."

"Neptune?!" Hamilton gasps. "That will be quite a journey!"

"Wish me luck, Professor," says Superman, grabbing Doomsday and soaring into the air.

The two foes travel through Earth's atmosphere and past the Moon. Doomsday sleeps through their long journey past the orbits of Mars, Jupiter, Saturn, and Uranus.

Eventually Superman spots a blue world in the distance. "I think I see Neptune, Professor," he says into his communicator. "What can you tell me about it?"

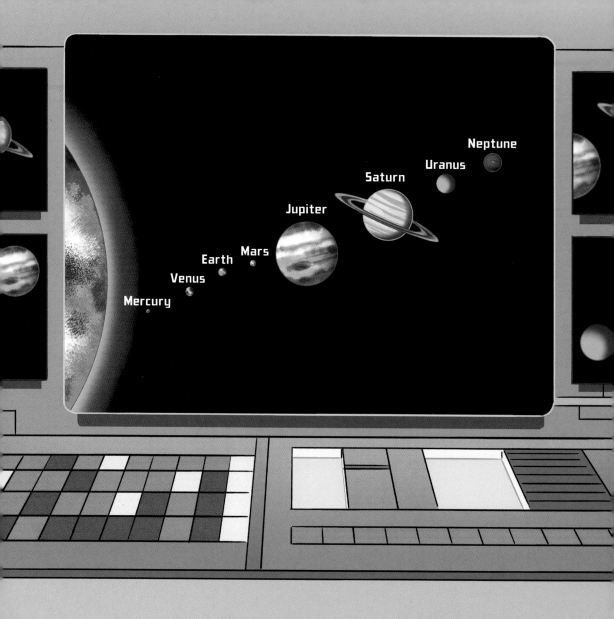

Professor Hamilton punches some buttons on his computer. A large diagram of the solar system fills his screen.

"Neptune is the eighth planet from the Sun," says Hamilton. "It's one of the four gas giants in our solar system—along with Jupiter, Saturn, and Uranus. Neptune is also 30 times farther from the Sun than Earth. Very little sunlight reaches this cold, dark planet."

"Interesting," says Superman. "It looks like a bright blue ball to me."

Hamilton pulls up a cross section of the planet on his screen.

"Large amounts of methane gas in the clouds and atmosphere give Neptune its color," he says. "The methane absorbs red light from the Sun, but it reflects blue light. The reflected light gives the planet its beautiful blue color."

"What's underneath all those clouds?" asks Superman.

"Like the other gas giants, Neptune has no solid surface," says Hamilton. "Its interior is a liquid ocean made up of water, ammonia, and methane. A solid core of rock and metal lies at the planet's center."

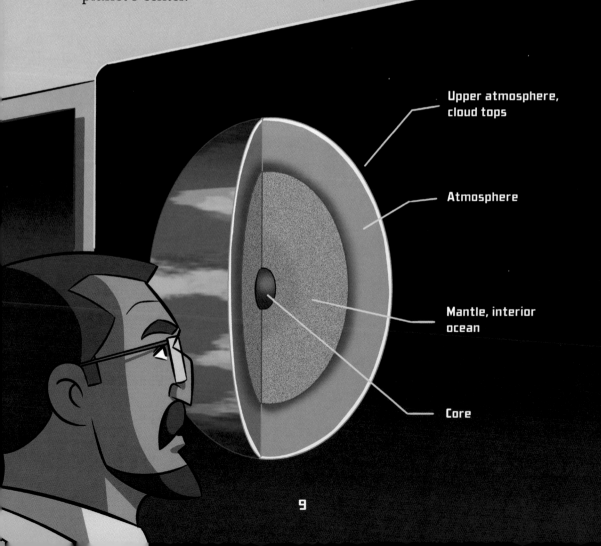

Upper atmosphere, cloud tops

Atmosphere

Mantle, interior ocean

Core

"Professor, I'm approaching some rings orbiting the planet," says Superman. "They look darker than the ones around Saturn."

"Saturn's rings contain a lot of ice, which reflects light from the Sun," says Hamilton. "Neptune's rings reflect less light because they are made mostly of dust and small rocks."

Just then, Doomsday's eyes open. The monster lets out a deep growl and forms his right hand into a fist.

Doomsday swings his massive right arm in a circle, punching Superman in the chest.

FACT

Neptune's rings were detected from Earth in 1984. Four years later, the *Voyager 2* spacecraft sent back the first photos of the planet's rings.

"Ooof!" groans Superman. His chest aches from Doomsday's powerful punch. He closes his eyes and begins to lose consciousness.

Neptune's gravity pulls Superman and Doomsday closer to the planet. Soon they fall through the planet's upper layer of frozen methane clouds. After that, they pass through the planet's atmosphere of hydrogen, helium, and methane.

They are rapidly approaching Neptune's interior ocean of water, ammonia, and methane.

FACT
The top of Neptune's atmosphere is very cold. It averages around minus 350 degrees Fahrenheit (minus 210 degrees Celsius).

"Superman, are you there?" calls out Professor Hamilton. "Can you hear me?"

When the Man of Steel fails to respond, a wide smile forms on Doomsday's face.

Fierce winds blow around Superman and Doomsday. The villain tightens his grip on Superman's wrist. The pressure causes the Man of Steel to gasp in pain.

Just as Superman opens his eyes, a violent storm rages around them.

Superman struggles to speak as winds crash against him.

Doomsday holds on tight, twisting his body to strike Superman with a razor-sharp arm bone.

"Professor, the winds . . . they're getting stronger," Superman says.

"Neptune's winds are the fastest in our solar system," says Hamilton. "They can reach speeds of 1,500 miles, or 2,400 kilometers, per hour."

As the winds increase around them, Superman and Doomsday tumble through the planet's soupy mix of chemicals. The Man of Steel dodges quickly to avoid Doomsday's dangerous spikes.

FACT

Voyager 2 discovered a storm the size of Earth on Neptune. Scientists named it the Great Dark Spot. The storm's winds were nine times stronger than Earth's most powerful hurricanes.

As quickly as the winds arrived, they suddenly die down. Superman surprises Doomsday by pulling the creature closer.

"Now it's time for you to take a nap!" declares the Man of Steel. He slams his right fist against Doomsday's head.

The monster groans and slips into unconsciousness again.

"Professor, it's getting hotter!" says Superman. "And the pressure is increasing as we sink deeper into the planet."

"You need to get out of there before you reach the planet's core, Superman," says Hamilton. "Scientists think that temperatures at the center of the core may top 9,000 degrees Fahrenheit, or 5,000 degrees Celsius."

"It's time to say goodbye to Neptune," says the Man of Steel as he carries Doomsday through the planet's upper atmosphere.

FACT
The pressure and temperature increase to very high levels deep within Neptune. These conditions cause the planet's methane to split into carbon and hydrogen. Scientists think this may create an ocean of diamonds around the planet's core.

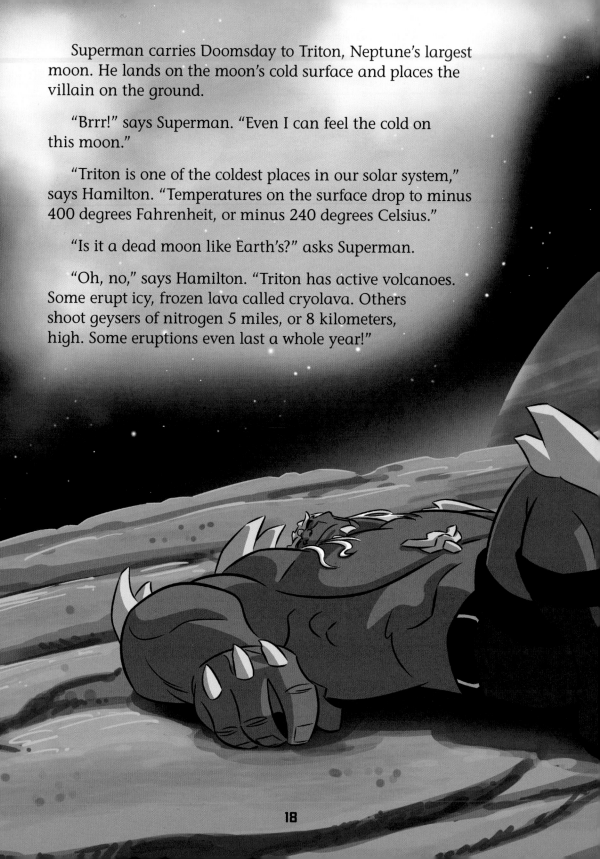

Superman carries Doomsday to Triton, Neptune's largest moon. He lands on the moon's cold surface and places the villain on the ground.

"Brrr!" says Superman. "Even I can feel the cold on this moon."

"Triton is one of the coldest places in our solar system," says Hamilton. "Temperatures on the surface drop to minus 400 degrees Fahrenheit, or minus 240 degrees Celsius."

"Is it a dead moon like Earth's?" asks Superman.

"Oh, no," says Hamilton. "Triton has active volcanoes. Some erupt icy, frozen lava called cryolava. Others shoot geysers of nitrogen 5 miles, or 8 kilometers, high. Some eruptions even last a whole year!"

FACT

Neptune has 14 moons. Six of them were discovered by the *Voyager 2* spacecraft in 1989.

"That gives me an idea, Professor," says Superman.

Suddenly, Doomsday's eyes snap open and he leaps to his feet.

The creature growls and leaps toward Superman.

"You'll have to move faster than that," says Superman as he flies away from Doomsday.

The monster jumps after the Man of Steel.

"Come and get me, Doomsday," says Superman, hovering above a tall, ice-covered mountain.

With an evil grin, the creature quickly climbs the mountain. He reaches out to grab Superman.

RUUUUUUUMBLE!

Suddenly, the mountain begins to shake.

"Too bad you slept through the professor's discussion about Triton," says Superman.

21

Superman soars out of the way as an icy stream of frozen lava erupts from the volcano.

Doomsday scrambles down the side of the volcano, but the icy lava quickly encases the monster.

WHOOOOSH!

Superman uses his super-breath to add several extra-thick layers of ice around Doomsday. The villain is now trapped—alive, but unable to move.

"Our solar system is not safe with Doomsday in it," says Superman. "I need to take him even farther away."

"Well, out beyond Neptune you'll find the Kuiper Belt. This ring of rocks, ice, and other bodies orbits the Sun," says Hamilton. "And even farther away is the Oort Cloud, which is where many comets exist. The Oort Cloud stretches halfway to the nearest star!"

"That sounds like a good place for Doomsday," says Superman. He lifts the frozen monster and soars high above Triton.

"You'll fly past the orbits of Pluto and the other frozen dwarf planets as you reach the Kuiper Belt," says Hamilton.

"Poor Pluto," says Superman. "I wish it was still considered a regular planet."

Hamilton chuckles. "A lot of people agree with you. But Pluto is smaller than Earth's moon. Starting in the 1990s, scientists discovered hundreds of other small Pluto-like bodies beyond Neptune. Now we call the largest ones dwarf planets."

FACT
A 24-year-old astronomer named Clyde Tombaugh discovered Pluto in 1930.

"Whoa!" says Superman. "A large chunk of dark ice just zoomed by!"

"The Kuiper Belt contains thousands of those ice-and-rock bodies," says Hamilton. "Some are more than 60 miles, or 100 kilometers, wide."

"How big is the Kuiper Belt?" asks Superman.

"The main belt is like a wide, flat disk," says Hamilton. "It's roughly 2 billion miles, or 3.2 billion kilometers, from inner edge to outer edge.

Superman's journey continues until he reaches the edge of the solar system. Another giant object zooms past him.

"Professor, an even bigger object just flew by me," says Superman.

"You must be in the Oort Cloud," says Hamilton. "That object was the central part of a comet. It's called the nucleus. A nucleus only becomes a bright comet if it orbits closer to the Sun."

"Well, this should be far enough," says Superman. He pushes the chunk of ice holding Doomsday into the Oort Cloud.

"Mission accomplished," says Superman. "I'm coming home now."

"You are now more than 10 trillion miles, or 16 trillion kilometers, away from Earth," Hamilton says.

"In that case, don't wait up for me, Professor," says Superman with a smile. "This trip might take me a while."

MORE ABOUT NEPTUNE

- Neptune was first discovered around 1845. Astronomers knew gravity from an unknown object was affecting Uranus' orbit. They used math to find Neptune's location before it was ever viewed with a telescope.

- Neptune is named after the Roman mythological god who ruled the oceans. The moon Triton is named after his son. All of the planet's other moons are named for relatives and subjects of Neptune.

- Neptune is the solar system's third largest planet, after Jupiter and Saturn. It has a diameter of about 30,000 miles (48,000 km). That's roughly four times wider than Earth.

- Neptune has very long years. Each orbit around the Sun takes approximately 165 Earth years.

- Like Earth, Neptune has four seasons. But each season on Neptune lasts about 40 years.

- NASA launched the *Voyager 2* spacecraft in 1977. It took 12 years to reach Neptune. It sent back more than 10,000 photos of the planet.

- Neptune's moon Triton may have once been part of the Kuiper Belt. If so, it was captured by Neptune's gravity and moved into orbit around the planet. Triton is about the same size as Pluto.

- Every year, Neptune's gravity pulls Triton a little closer. In a few million years, Triton may get too close and be broken into pieces. When that happens, it may even become a ring around Neptune.

- Scientists estimate that the Oort Cloud may contain more than 1 trillion comets.

- Pluto was named by Venetia Burney of Oxford, England. She was 11 years old when she won a worldwide contest to name it.

- The *New Horizons* spacecraft flew past Pluto in 2015. It is now traveling 1 billion miles (1.6 billion km) beyond Pluto to reach another object in the Kuiper Belt in 2019.

GLOSSARY

ammonia (uh-moh-NEE-uh)—a gas that is made up of nitrogen and hydrogen

asteroid (AS-tuh-royd)—a large space rock that moves around the Sun

astronomer (uh-STRAH-nuh-muhr)—a scientist who studies stars, planets, and other objects in space

atmosphere (AT-muhss-fihr)—the layer of gases that surrounds some planets, dwarf planets, and moons

comet (KOM-uht)—a ball of rock and ice that orbits the Sun

core (KOR)—the inner part of a planet or a dwarf planet that is made of metal or rock

cryolava (KRY-oh-lava)—an icy substance consisting of water, ammonia, or methane that erupts from ice volcanoes on some moons in the solar system

geyser (GYE-zur)—an underground spring that shoots hot liquid and steam through a hole in the ground

gravity (GRAV-uh-tee)—a force that pulls objects together

methane (meth-AYN)—a colorless, flammable gas; methane becomes a liquid at extremely cold temperatures

orbit (OR-bit)—the path an object follows while circling another object in space

READ MORE

Adamson, Thomas K. *The Secrets of Neptune.* Smithsonian Planets. North Mankato, Minn.: Capstone Press, 2016.

Black, Vanessa. *Neptune.* Space Voyager. Minneapolis: Bullfrog Books, 2018.

Brockman, Noah. *Journey to Neptune.* Spotlight on Space Science. New York: PowerKids Press, 2015.

TITLES IN THIS SET

INDEX

INTERNET SITES

Use FactHound to find Internet sites related to this book.
Visit *www.facthound.com*
Just type in 9781543515749 and go.

Published by Capstone Press in 2018
1710 Roe Crest Drive
North Mankato, Minnesota 56003
www.mycapstone.com

Cataloging-in-publication information is on file with the Library of Congress.
ISBN 978-1-5435-1574-9 (library binding)
ISBN 978-1-5435-1582-4 (paperback)
ISBN 978-1-5435-1590-9 (eBook PDF)

Editorial Credits
Christopher Harbo, editor; Kayla Rossow, designer; Laura Manthe, production specialist

Summary: Superman squares off against the super-villain Doomsday in an adventure that reveals
the remarkable features and characteristics of Neptune and the outer edges of the solar system.

Illustration Credits
Gregg Schigiel (Superman): back cover, 1, 32

Printed in the United States of America.
PA0174